# Pizza, Bread, and Savory Tarts

Published originally in Italian as *Pizza, focacce e torte salate*
© 2005 Food Editore srl
Via Bordoni, 8 - 20124 MILAN, ITALY
Via Mazzini, 6 - 43100 PARMA, ITALY

**English Translation**
Traduzioni Culinarie

**Photographs**
Alberto Rossi and Davide Di Prato

**Recipes**
Simone Rugiati and Licia Cagnoni

**Thanks to**
I Love My House (Barazzoni, Parma)

This 2008 edition printed exclusively for Barnes & Noble, Inc.,
by Food Editore srl.

ISBN-13: 978-1-4351-0621-5

Printed and bound in China
10  9  8  7  6  5  4  3  2  1

# Pizza, Bread, and Savory Tarts

Great Recipes from the Chefs of Food Editore

FOOD
EDITORE

Parma, Milan

# Contents

# Basic Techniques

## PIZZA & CO.: A BRIEF HISTORY

Pizza, focaccia, and savory tarts are all variations on a single original recipe that has evolved through countless refinements. The first mixture of water and wheat flour was made more than 3,000 years ago. It was a basic dough that first was simply baked, and then later left to rise before baking.

Even before the relatively recent invention of pizza in Naples, pizza-like flatbreads and focaccias had been enjoyed in ancient Greece and Rome and all around the Mediterranean.

The most famous pizza, the archetype, is the Neapolitan pizza which was created between the eighteenth and nineteenth centuries in Naples; this is the one with mozzarella cheese and tomatoes (the tomato having become available in Europe only after Columbus's New World explorations). Pizza has a fascinating history and serves in some ways as a symbol of the vitality that has always characterized Naples and its inhabitants.

There is a famous anecdote about how the classic pizza Margherita was invented. According to tradition, in 1889, pizza-maker Raffaele Esposito created a pizza for the Italian Queen Margherita. He topped it with white mozzarella cheese, red tomato, and green basil, echoing the Italian flag, and dedicated the pizza to the queen.

Pizza actually started out as a food for the common people, made of simple,

inexpensive, yet wholesome ingredients that are all part of what's known as the "Mediterranean diet." Pizza was cooked in bakeries around the city, then sold directly in the streets or delivered to homes.

Pizza spread to the United States and many other countries via the pizza-makers who emigrated in search of better living conditions. These people brought their secrets with them and found great success. Today despite regional differences and innovations, pizza is still one of the world's most popular dishes.

Some form of pizza is prepared and eaten in countries all over the world, and almost anywhere you travel, the word "pizza" will be understood.

# BASIC INGREDIENTS

**Flour** Wheat flour is used for pizza dough because it makes the dough easy to knead, soft, and elastic. Bread flour, which contains many proteins and is recommended for long rising periods, can also be added. Another alternative is special pizza flour, which already contains the correct mix of flours and is available from large or high-end supermarkets.

**Water** When it comes to water, temperature is important, as it affects the speed of rising. If the water is too cold, especially in winter, the rising process is slower. However, if the water is too hot, the rising will occur at an accelerated rate and the dough will be less elastic. The ideal water temperature is about 72°F in the winter and 64°F in the summer.

**Yeasts** These are living microorganisms that produce the gases needed for the dough to ferment.

Fresh brewer's yeast is the type best suited to homemade pizza, but it has a very short shelf life. Active dry yeast can also be used with good results. In either case, the yeast must be dissolved in lukewarm water before mixing it with the flour.

**Tomatoes** These are a key pizza ingredient. Traditionally, canned and peeled tomatoes are pureed and seasoned with oil, salt, pepper, and oregano. The sauce is then spread on the pizza base before baking. Some cooks add a teaspoon of sugar to the sauce to reduce the acidity. In the summer, fresh diced tomatoes can be used instead of canned ones.

## PIZZA

**Makes 1 pound pizza dough**

4 teaspoons active dry yeast

1 cup lukewarm water

1 teaspoon salt

1 teaspoon sugar

6 tablespoons extra-virgin olive oil

1 1/3 cups (6 ounces) all-purpose flour

3/4 cup (4 ounces) bread flour

## Method

Dissolve the yeast in the lukewarm water. Add the salt, sugar, and olive oil and mix thoroughly with a wooden spoon.

Sift the flours together and mound them on a work surface. Form a well in the center and add the liquid. Mix to form a dough and knead well. Form a ball, coat in flour, and place in a large floured plastic bowl. Cover with a clean kitchen towel and let rest for about 2 hours.

Knead the dough again briefly, then shape into single-portion balls. Let rise under a kitchen towel for 1 hour.

### Variations

For a browner, crispier crust, add an egg yolk to the dough. The crust can also be varied by adding 1 cup (5½ ounces) boiled and mashed potatoes to every 4 cups (1 pound, 2 ounces) of flour. This dough is particularly suited for pan-fried pizzas and focaccias.

Too much salt can hinder the dough's fermentation. A tablespoon of malt extract or a pinch of sugar can help improve rising, and give the dough a distinctive flavor.

For whole-wheat pizza dough, mix 4 cups (1 pound, 2 ounces) whole-wheat flour, 4 teaspoons yeast, 2 tablespoons olive oil, and salt. Add enough water to make a smooth dough and knead for about 10 minutes, until the dough comes away cleanly from the work surface. Shape the dough into a ball and let rise in a warm place for about 1½ hours.

### Cooking

The wood-fired or electric ovens used in pizzerias can reach much higher temperatures than regular home ovens. On a baking surface heated to 570° to 660°F, pizza cooks evenly in about 10 minutes, while in a home oven, it can take more than 20 minutes. The extra time in the oven affects the rising of the pizza. Because their high temperatures make for speedy cooking, wood-fired ovens are particularly suited to baking thin pizzas, while home ovens are

generally better for pizzas with thicker crusts. Some people suggest putting a small saucepan of water (about 4 cups) in the oven along with the pizza to stop the dough from getting too dry.

After rolling the dough out on the baking sheet, spread the tomato sauce over it, but add the mozzarella only halfway through the cooking process, to avoid burning the cheese.

### FOCACCIA

Focaccia is a flatbread, a forerunner of pizza, and bears many similarities to it. Pizza was supposedly invented to improve upon focaccia's plain toppings, but today there are many tasty and imaginative recipes for focaccia. While focaccia can't replace a complete meal, it can make a tasty snack.

**Makes 1 pound, 9 ounces focaccia dough**

4 ½ teaspoons (1 ounce) active dry yeast
4 cups bread flour
¼ cup (½ stick) butter
olive oil
1 teaspoon salt

## Method

Dissolve the yeast in a little lukewarm water, then add the remaining ingredients and knead thoroughly to create a dough. Let rest in a warm place, covered or oiled, for about 15 minutes.

Cut the dough into portions, shape into balls, and let rest for a few more minutes. Arrange the dough balls on a baking sheet, flatten them out, and brush with olive oil. Let the dough rise for another 30 minutes, then bake at 480°F. Cooking time will vary depending on the dough's thickness and size.

## Variations

For a tastier and richer focaccia, use lard instead of butter.

## Tips

If you want a thicker focaccia to stuff with different fillings, bake it at a temperature 85°F lower than the recommended one; after 10 minutes, reduce it again. This gives the yeast more time to puff up the dough.

## PUFF PASTRY

This light and flaky pastry makes an ideal base for many recipes.

**Makes 1 pound, 2 ounces puff pastry dough**

1⅔ cups (7 ounces) all-purpose flour
7 tablespoons water
1 pinch salt
1 cup (9 ounces) butter, cut into
  small pieces

## Method

Mound the flour on a work surface, make a well in the center, and then add the water and salt. Mix together until smooth, then wrap in a clean kitchen towel and let rest for about 20 minutes.

Using a rolling pin, roll the dough out to form a square ¼-inch thick. Place the butter in the middle, fold the dough over, and close it completely, forming a parcel. Roll out gently with the rolling pin, then wrap the dough in foil and refrigerate for 5 minutes.

Unwrap the dough and place on the work surface. Roll the dough out into a long strip about ½-inch thick. Fold a third in toward the middle, then cover it with another third, to form three layers of dough. Turn it around 90 degrees, then roll the dough out again into a long strip. Fold it again in thirds, then wrap in foil and refrigerate for about 30 minutes. Repeat two more times.

When finished, leave the dough to rest in the refrigerator for at least an hour before using.

## PIADINA

A tortilla-like flatbread from Romagna, the piadina has a long pedigree, with references dating back to the Middle Ages.

Piadina are perfect accompaniments to salami, cheese, and vegetables. As with focaccia and savory tarts, the only limits on possible fillings are your taste and your imagination.

## Makes 1 pound, 2 ounces piadina dough

4 cups (1 pound, 2 ounces) all-purpose
  flour
3 tablespoons lard
1 cup warm water plus extra
salt

### Method

Mound the flour on a work surface. Dissolve the lard in the warm water and stir in a generous pinch of salt. Make a well in the middle of the flour and pour in the lard mixture. Work into a dough using your fingertips, then knead to form a smooth and elastic ball. If necessary, add more lukewarm water. Wrap the dough in plastic wrap and let rest at room temperature.

   Using a rolling pin, roll out small pieces of dough to a thickness of 1/8 inch. Cook on a very hot cast-iron griddle for about 3 minutes on each side, turning as soon as brown bubbles form.

### Variations

For a puffier piadina, add 1 teaspoon baking soda and a drizzle of olive oil to the dough.

### Tips

The thinner the dough is rolled out, the crispier the piadina will be.

### PANZEROTTO

This dish is yet another creation from Naples. The name panzerotto comes from Naples, although panzerotti can also refer to potato croquettes and a type of pasta.

   As with pizza, panzerotti are highly popular throughout the Mediterranean region, with slight variations.

## Makes 11 ounces panzerotto dough

1 1/2 teaspoons (1/4 ounce) active
  dry yeast
7 tablespoons lukewarm water
salt
1 tablespoon extra-virgin olive oil
1 2/3 cups (7 ounces) all-purpose flour,
  sifted

### Method

Dissolve the yeast in the lukewarm water. Add a generous pinch of salt and the extra-virgin olive oil. Pour the liquid into the sifted flour, and work the ingredients with the fingertips to create a dough.

   Knead vigorously until the dough is smooth, then let rise in a warm place, covered with a damp kitchen towel, for about 30 minutes.

## Variations

The panzerotti dough can be flavored with finely chopped aromatic herbs or a mixture of finely chopped walnuts, hazelnuts, and/or pistachios.

## BREAD

Bread, a universal symbol for food, has a very long history. The two elements that perhaps most distinguish modern bread from that baked by ancient peoples are the rising process and the use of soft-wheat flour. The Egyptians were the first to bake "modern" bread, which then spread around the Mediterranean basin.

Bread made its first appearance in Rome relatively late, in the second century B.C.E.; however, the Romans had been eating flatbreads for some time. In Greece at this same time, different types of bread had already been present for at least a century.

Today it is hard to imagine a life without bread, baked in many different ways and available in many different shapes. Various types of leavened bread can be found in northern Italy, with an apparently Celtic legacy, while in central and southern Italy, including the islands, bread often takes unusual shapes, and breads with a very rustic appearance and minimal rising are quite common.

Here is a basic bread recipe:

### Makes 1 pound, 9 ounces dough

4 ½ teaspoons (1 ounce) active dry
  yeast
4 cups (1 pound, 2 ounces) all-purpose
  flour
water
½ cup (1 stick) butter
salt

## Method

Dissolve the yeast in a little warm water. Mix the yeast and water with two tablespoons of the flour, then knead until smooth. Form into a ball, cut a cross on top, and let rise until doubled in volume.

Mix the remaining flour, butter, a pinch of salt, and enough water to form another dough. Add the two doughs together and knead vigorously until small bubbles appear on the surface. Form into a ball, cut a cross on top, and let rise until doubled in volume.

# Pizzas

The following pages feature
tasty pizzas with both simple
and luxurious toppings,
including new ideas
for this classic staple
of Italian cuisine.

# Calabrian Pizza with Capers and Eggplant

**Serves 4**

### Dough
1 pound pizza dough (see page 8)

### Topping
1 eggplant, sliced
1¼ cups (10 ounces) diced buffalo mozzarella
1 tablespoon capers, drained and rinsed
20 cherry tomatoes, quartered
3 tablespoons extra-virgin olive oil
salt and pepper
fresh basil leaves, torn


**Preparation time** 20 minutes
**Cooking time** 15 minutes
**Level** easy
**Beer** Italian lager


Preheat oven to 450°F. If using a pizza stone, place it in the oven when you preheat.

For individual round pizzas, divide the pizza dough into 4 balls. For a square pizza, stretch the dough in an oiled rectangular baking tray. Cover the dough with a damp cloth and let rise.

Heat a cast-iron grill pan and grill the eggplant slices for 2 minutes on each side.

If making round pizzas, roll the dough balls out into thin discs. Place the pizza bases on an oiled baking sheet or hot pizza stone. Top with mozzarella, capers, and tomatoes and season with olive oil, salt, and pepper. Bake for 8 minutes.

Add the eggplant slices to the top of the pizza and continue baking until the edges of the crust are browned and crispy. Remove from the oven, sprinkle with basil, and serve immediately.

**Cook's tip** For a thicker pizza, roll out the dough in an oiled baking tray; top with tomatoes, capers, and mozzarella; and let rise in a warm place. Bake for 12 minutes in an oven that has been preheated to 425°F, adding eggplant halfway through.

# Pizza with Fresh Tomatoes and Artichoke Hearts

**Serves 4**

### Dough
1 pound pizza dough (see page 8)

### Topping
1½ cups (12 ounces) diced buffalo mozzarella
2 tomatoes, thinly sliced
salt and pepper
2 tablespoons extra-virgin olive oil
1 cup (7 ounces) artichoke hearts in oil, drained, dried, and cut into wedges
fresh basil leaves

**Preparation time** 15 minutes
**Cooking time** 10 minutes
**Level** easy
**Beer** Italian Lager

Preheat oven to 450°F.

Roll out the dough on a floured work surface until thin, then top with the mozzarella and the tomato slices. Season to taste with salt and pepper and drizzle with extra-virgin olive oil.

Add the artichoke hearts and bake for 8 minutes, or until the crust is cooked through. Remove from the oven and sprinkle with fresh basil leaves. Serve immediately.

# Mushroom and Shrimp Pizza

**Serves 4**

### *Dough*
1 pound pizza dough (see page 8)

### *Topping*
4 white button mushrooms
1 cup (7 ounces) diced mozzarella
15 shrimp, peeled and deveined
20 black olives, drained, rinsed, and pitted
3 tablespoons extra-virgin olive oil
salt and pepper
1 bunch arugula, chopped

**Preparation time** 20 minutes
**Cooking time** 15 minutes
**Level** easy
**Beer** Irish stout

Preheat oven to 450°F.

Divide the dough into 4 balls and let rise under a damp cloth in a warm place for about two hours.

Wipe the mushrooms clean with a damp paper towel, cut off the earthy part of the stalk, and thinly slice the rest.

Roll the dough out thinly into 4 rounds, then top them with mozzarella, shrimp, olives, and mushroom slices. Drizzle with olive oil and sprinkle with salt and pepper.

Bake for about 8 minutes, or until the crust is cooked through, then sprinkle with the chopped arugula. Season again with a drizzle of olive oil, and a pinch of salt. Serve immediately.

# Pizza with Fava Beans, Pecorino, and Pancetta

**PANCETTA**

Pancetta is a cured meat made from fatty pork belly. Similar types of cured meats are made in many countries around the world. Pancetta comes in many forms, the most common being *tesa* (stretched) and *arrotolata* (rolled). Pancetta tesa is stretched, trimmed, salted, and then smoked or cured; pancetta arrotolata is obtained from the leaner pieces, which are rolled up, tied, and then cured. A third type of pancetta is referred to as pancetta coppata—pork fat rolled around a piece of neck meat and then aged.

Serves 4

**Dough**
1 pound pizza dough (see page 8)

**Topping**
1 ½ cùps (11 ounces) shelled fava beans
9 ounces pecorino cheese, grated
3 tablespoons extra-virgin olive oil
salt and black pepper
5 ½ ounces pancetta, thinly sliced

**Preparation time** 20 minutes
**Cooking time** 10 minutes
**Level** easy
**Beer** Czech Pilsner

Preheat oven to 475°F.

Divide the dough into 4 balls and leave to rise under a damp cloth.

Blanch the fava beans in salted boiling water for 1 minute, then drain and rinse in cold water. Remove the outer skins.

Roll out the dough with a rolling pin or stretch out by hand on a floured surface, giving the dough a round shape. Top with the fava beans and pecorino cheese. Season with a drizzle of olive oil and pinches of salt and black pepper.

Bake for about 6 minutes. Remove from oven as soon as pizza crust is slightly browned and cooked through. Lay the pancetta slices on top of pizza and serve immediately.

**Cook's tip** This pizza is traditionally prepared for May Day celebrations in Tuscany. The pancetta slices melt slightly when placed on top of the hot pizza.

# Pizza with Artichokes and Sun-Dried Tomatoes

**Serves 4**

### Dough
4 cups (1 pound, 1½ ounces) whole-wheat flour
4 teaspoons active dry yeast
2 tablespoons extra-virgin olive oil
water

### Topping
7 ounces mozzarella, cubed
10½ ounces baby artichokes in oil, cut into wedges
1 oregano sprig, leaves removed
pepper
3 tablespoons extra-virgin olive oil
20 sun-dried cherry tomatoes in oil, drained

**Preparation time** 15 minutes
**Cooking time** 20 minutes
**Level** easy
**Beer** Irish stout

Mix together the flour, yeast, and olive oil with enough water to form a smooth dough that pulls easily away from the work surface. Form into a ball and let rise in a warm place for 1½ hours.

Preheat oven to 400°F.

Divide the dough in half and roll out into 2 circles about ¼-inch thick. Place them on two round baking trays, each 11 inches in diameter.

Pat the mozzarella cubes dry with a paper towel. Scatter the artichoke wedges, mozzarella cubes, and oregano leaves over the pizza bases, sprinkle with pepper, and drizzle with olive oil.

Bake in the oven for about 15 minutes, then top with the sun-dried cherry tomatoes and return to the oven for another 5 minutes.

# Pizza with Sun-Dried Tomatoes and Arugula

**Serves 4**

### Dough
1 pound pizza dough (see page 8)

### Topping
1½ cups (11 ounces) diced mozzarella
20 sun-dried cherry tomatoes in oil, drained
salt
2 bunches arugula, chopped
5½ ounces Parmesan, shaved
3 tablespoons extra-virgin olive oil

**Preparation time** 10 minutes
**Cooking time** 15 minutes
**Level** easy
**Beer** German Pilsner

Preheat oven to 425°F.

Using a rolling pin, roll out the dough on a lightly floured work surface. Sprinkle the mozzarella cheese over the pizza dough. Arrange the sun-dried tomatoes on top. Season to taste with salt and bake for 15 minutes, or until the crust is cooked through.

Before serving, sprinkle with the arugula and Parmesan and drizzle with the extra-virgin olive oil.

# White Pizza with Truffle Oil

**Serves 4**

### *Dough*
1 pound pizza dough (see page 8)

### *Topping*
2 fresh porcini mushrooms or 4 ounces porcini in oil
3 tablespoons truffle oil
salt
1 cup (7 ounces) diced mozzarella
5 ounces Parmesan, shaved

**Preparation time** 10 minutes
**Cooking time** 10 minutes
**Level** easy
**Beer** English pale ale

Preheat oven to 450°F.

Cut off the earthy part of the mushroom stalk and wipe the mushrooms clean with a damp paper towel. Cut the mushrooms in half lengthwise, then slice them. If using porcini in oil, drain and pat dry with a paper towel.

Divide the dough into 4 portions and roll them out into rounds. Drizzle with truffle oil and season with salt. Top with the mozzarella and porcini. Sprinkle with the Parmesan, then bake for 8 minutes, or until the crust is cooked through. Serve immediately.

**Cook's tip** The heady fragrance of the truffle oil perfumes the whole pizza and, together with the porcini, creates a harmony of woodsy flavors.

# Truffle, Provolone, and Ham Pizza

**HAM**

The best cooked ham (as opposed to prosciutto, which is dry-cured, not cooked) is made from a deboned leg of pork, which is cured in brine and then steamed in a special mold. Once cooled in the mold, the ham needs a brief aging period (just a few days) before it is ready to be eaten.

**Serves 4**

**Dough**
1 pound pizza dough (see page 8)

**Topping**
9 ounces mild provola cheese
  or sharp provolone, grated
½ cup (3½ ounces) chopped
  mozzarella
2 tablespoons extra-virgin olive oil
salt
6½ ounces ham, thinly sliced,
  then cut into strips
1 small black truffle, shaved

**Preparation time** 10 minutes
**Cooking time** 12 minutes
**Level** easy
**Beer** German Weizen

Preheat oven to 475°F.

Divide the dough into 4 balls and let rise in a warm place under a damp cloth for about two hours.

Mix together the two cheeses.

Stretch or roll out the dough on a floured work surface, making it as thin as possible, then top with the cheese mixture. Season the edges with a little olive oil and salt, then place the ham strips on top of the whole pizza.

Bake for 8 minutes, or until the crust is cooked through.

Remove the pizza from the oven as soon as the edges are browned and crispy. Arrange on serving plates, sprinkle with truffle shavings, and serve immediately.

**Cook's tip** The intense flavor of the provola cheese pairs well with the pungent black truffle fragrance to create a deliciously indulgent pizza.

# Sardinian-Style Pizza

**Serves 4**

4 sheets pane carasau or Armenian cracker bread
½ cup crushed tomatoes
1 cup (7 ounces) diced mozzarella
2 tablespoons capers
⅓ cup (2 ounces) black olives
oregano
salt
4 tablespoons extra-virgin olive oil
3½ ounces Sardinian pecorino cheese, shaved

**Preparation time** 10 minutes
**Cooking time** 10 minutes
**Level** easy
**Beer** German Weizen

Preheat the oven to 400°F.

Spread 3 tablespoons of tomatoes evenly over each sheet of bread. Top each one with mozzarella, capers, olives, oregano, a pinch of salt, a drizzle of olive oil, and a layer of pecorino shavings. Place on baking sheets and bake for about 10 minutes. Serve immediately.

**Cook's tip** Add a few anchovy fillets or grilled eggplant slices for a heartier variation.

# Pizza with Sausage and Greens

**Serves 4**

### Dough
1 pound pizza dough (see page 8)

### Topping
1 bunch bitter greens (turnip tops or broccoli rabe), stalks removed
2 pork sausages
3 tablespoons extra-virgin olive oil
½ dried red chili pepper, crumbled
2 garlic cloves, smashed
salt and pepper

**Preparation time** 20 minutes
**Cooking time** 25 minutes
**Level** easy
**Beer** English pale ale

Preheat oven to 425°F.

Wash the greens, then drain, leaving some water on the leaves.

Heat a little water in a frying pan and cook the sausages for about 5 minutes. Drain and set aside.

Heat the olive oil and chili pepper in a frying pan, then add the garlic and sauté until browned. Add the wet greens and cover. Cook for 5 minutes, stirring occasionally.

Halve the sausages and add to the pan with the greens. Season to taste with salt and pepper, and cook for another 8 minutes.

Stretch or roll out the dough, leaving it quite thick, then let rise in an oiled pan in a warm place for about two hours.

Top the risen dough with the greens and crumble the sausages over them. Bake for 12 minutes, or until the crust is cooked through.

Remove from the oven and serve hot.

**Cook's tip** To enrich the pizza and make the crust softer, knead thin slices of mozzarella into the pizza dough before rolling.

# Radicchio and Parmesan Pizza

Serves 4 to 6

### Dough
4 teaspoons active dry yeast
$^2/_3$ cup lukewarm water
3 tablespoons extra-virgin olive oil
2$^1/_2$ cups (11 ounces) all-purpose flour plus extra for dusting
$^3/_4$ cup (3$^1/_2$ ounces) bread flour
salt

### Topping
4 tablespoons extra-virgin olive oil
2 cups (14 ounces) shredded radicchio
salt and freshly ground black pepper
2 to 3 tablespoons balsamic vinegar
1 tablespoon chopped parsley
5 ounces Parmesan, shaved

**Preparation time** 15 minutes
**Cooking time** 30 minutes
**Level** easy
**Beer** Belgian white

Dissolve the yeast in a little of the lukewarm water. Add the olive oil and 2 tablespoons of all-purpose flour, and stir until thick. Let rise in a warm place for 30 minutes.

Mound the remaining all-purpose flour and the bread flour on a wooden pastry board and make a well in the center. Place risen starter dough in the middle, add salt, and gradually pour in enough of the lukewarm water to form a soft dough. Knead vigorously for 10 minutes, shape into a ball, dust with flour, and cover with a cloth. Let rise in a warm place for about 2 hours.

Preheat oven to 400°F.

Divide the dough into 2 parts. Roll or stretch out each portion of dough into a round about ¼-inch thick.

Brush two baking sheets with olive oil and place the dough on them. Fold the round inward around the edges to make a thick border. Bake for 15 minutes.

Meanwhile, heat 2 tablespoons of olive oil and sauté the radicchio with a pinch of salt. Add the balsamic vinegar, then the parsley. Spread the radicchio over the pizza bases, then return them to the oven for 10 minutes.

Remove from the oven, top with the Parmesan shavings, sprinkle with freshly ground pepper, and finish with a drizzle of extra-virgin olive oil.

# Mini Potato Pizzas with Vegetables and Tomatoes

**Serves 4**

### *Dough*
4 teaspoons active dry yeast
7 tablespoons milk
2 cups (9 ounces) all-purpose flour
1 small potato (about 4 ounces), boiled and mashed
2 tablespoons extra-virgin olive oil

### *Topping*
1 cup (5 ounces) cherry tomatoes
extra-virgin olive oil
salt and pepper
oregano
1 cup (5 ounces) grilled eggplant and zucchini in oil
1 cup (5 ounces) chopped buffalo mozzarella

**Preparation time** 15 minutes
**Cooking time** 35 minutes
**Level** easy
**Beer** Italian lager

Preheat oven to 350°F.

Dissolve the yeast in the milk, then add all of the other ingredients for the dough and knead until smooth. Shape into a ball, cover with a clean kitchen towel, and let rise for about 1 hour.

Meanwhile, place the cherry tomatoes on a baking tray, brush with olive oil, and sprinkle with salt, pepper, and oregano. Bake for 15 minutes. Remove from the oven and raise the oven temperature to 375°F.

Roll out the dough and cut into small circles about 3¼ inches in diameter. Place the circles on a baking tray and let rise for 15 minutes.

Bake the mini pizzas for 15 minutes, then top with the cherry tomatoes, grilled eggplant and zucchini, and mozzarella. Bake again for 5 minutes.

**Variation** The mini pizzas may also be topped with mozzarella cheese, a drizzle of basil pesto, onions cooked with thyme, grilled peppers, goat cheese, and cubes of avocado and tomato.

# Spicy Pizza with Bitter Greens

**CHILI PEPPER**

Sweet bell peppers and hot chili peppers are botanically very similar. The main difference, apart from their size, is that the chili peppers possess a higher quantity of capsaicin (the active component that gives them their characteristic spiciness).

**Serves 4 to 6**

### *Dough*

4 teaspoons active dry yeast

²/₃ cup lukewarm water

2½ cups (11 ounces) all-purpose flour plus extra for dusting

¾ cup (3½ ounces) bread flour

salt

3 tablespoons extra-virgin olive oil

### *Topping*

4 tablespoons extra-virgin olive oil

2 garlic cloves, thinly sliced

1 dried red chili pepper

2 cups (14 ounces) bitter greens (turnip tops or broccoli rabe), washed

salt

1 cup (5 ounces) chopped buffalo mozzarella

*Preparation time* 30 minutes
*Cooking time* 30 minutes
*Level* easy
*Beer* German Weizen

Dissolve the yeast in a little of the lukewarm water. Add 2 tablespoons of the all-purpose flour and stir to make a thick batter. Let rise in a warm place for 30 minutes.

Mound the remaining all-purpose flour and the bread flour onto a work surface and make a well in the center. Place the risen starter dough in the middle, add salt, and gradually pour in enough of the lukewarm water to obtain a soft dough. Knead vigorously for 10 minutes, shape into a ball, dust with flour, and cover with a clean kitchen towel. Let rise in a warm place for about 2 hours.

Preheat oven to 400°F.

With a rolling pin, roll the dough in a rectangle the same size as the baking sheet and about ¼-inch thick.

Brush the baking sheet with olive oil and line it with the dough, forming a slightly higher border around the edges.

Heat the olive oil for the topping with the garlic and chili pepper, then sauté the greens. Add salt and a little water, then cover and cook for 10 minutes until tender.

Spread the greens over the dough, top with the buffalo mozzarella, and bake for 20 minutes.

# Whole-Wheat Pizza with Vegetables

**Serves 4**

### Dough
4 teaspoons active dry yeast
½ teaspoon sugar
¾ cup plus 1 tablespoon lukewarm water
1²/₃ cups (7 ounces) whole-wheat flour
1²/₃ cups (7 ounces) all-purpose flour
4 tablespoons extra-virgin olive oil
salt and pepper

### Topping
1 red onion, sliced
1 zucchini, thinly sliced
½ yellow bell pepper, julienned
½ red bell pepper, julienned
extra-virgin olive oil
salt and pepper

**Preparation time** 20 minutes
**Cooking time** 30 minutes
**Level** easy
**Beer** Belgian White

Dissolve the yeast and sugar in the lukewarm water, then mix together with the two flours. Add the olive oil and knead. Shape the dough into a ball and let rest for 2 hours.

Roll or stretch out the dough, leaving it quite thick. Arrange all the vegetables on the dough and drizzle with extra-virgin olive oil. Add pinches of salt and pepper. Let rise again for 1 hour.

Preheat oven to 375°F. Bake pizza for 20 minutes, or until the crust is cooked through. Serve hot.

# Savory Tarts

This chapter offers delicious recipes for savory tarts that are sure to impress. Amaze your guests and satisfy even the most demanding palates with fish, meat, cheese, or vegetable tarts.

# Onion and Goat Cheese Tart

**Serves 4**

### Dough
4 teaspoons active dry yeast
2 cups (9 ounces) all-purpose flour
1/3 cup plus 1 tablespoon (2 ounces) farro (emmer) flour
2 tablespoons extra-virgin olive oil
salt

### Filling
2 tablespoons extra-virgin olive oil
4 white onions, thinly sliced
salt
3 tablespoons Vin Santo or other sweet dessert wine
3 slices of white sandwich bread
1/4 cup plus 3 tablespoons milk
4 ounces fresh goat cheese

**Preparation time**  30 minutes
**Cooking time** 40 minutes
**Level** medium
**Wine** well-structured, dry white with intense, full flavors,
such as Friuli Malvasia Istriana

Preheat the oven to 375°F. Dissolve the yeast in a little warm water and let sit for 10 minutes. Mix the 2 flours together and mound them on a work surface. Make a well in the center and add the olive oil, salt, yeast mixture, and enough water to form a smooth and compact dough. Work the dough quickly, roll into a ball, and let rest for 20 minutes at room temperature.

Heat the olive oil in a frying pan and add the onions. Brown briefly, season with salt, and add the Vin Santo. Cover and cook over low heat until the onions are transparent and soft. Remove from the heat and cool.

Soak the bread in the milk, drain, and squeeze out the excess liquid. Crumble the bread over the goat cheese and mix well with a fork. Stir the onions into the cheese mixture.

Roll out the dough into a thin sheet and place it in a 9 1/2-inch baking dish lined with parchment paper. Spread the onion mixture over the dough and bake for 25 minutes. Serve warm.

# Zucchini and Escarole Tart

**Serves 4**

4 tablespoons extra-virgin olive oil
1 garlic clove, smashed
1 head of escarole, washed and coarsely chopped
salt and pepper
1 roll phyllo dough
2 zucchini, sliced

***Preparation time*** 20 minutes
***Cooking time*** 25 minutes
***Level*** easy
***Wine*** medium-bodied white with a bouquet of mature yellow fruit,
such as Tuscany Chardonnay

Preheat oven to 400°F.

Heat 2 tablespoons of the olive oil in a large frying pan with the smashed garlic clove. Add the escarole, cover, and cook for 10 minutes until soft. Remove the garlic and season to taste with salt and pepper. Drain off any excess liquid.

Spread out three sheets of phyllo dough on a lightly greased baking sheet. Evenly spread the escarole over the dough, then top with the sliced zucchini.

Season the tart with pinches of salt and pepper and drizzle with extra-virgin olive oil. Cover with 2 sheets of phyllo dough and bake for 12 to 15 minutes, or until the crust is golden brown. Serve immediately.

***Cook's tip*** Phyllo is an extremely thin pastry dough. It has a very short cooking time whether it is baked or fried. It is ideal for appetizers, meat, fish, vegetables or sweets.

# Savory Tart with Ham, Eggs, and Cheese

**Serves 4**

9 ounces puff pastry (see page 10) or packaged frozen puff pastry, thawed
7 ounces ham, thinly sliced
5½ ounces fontina, thinly sliced
3 eggs
salt
6 tablespoons heavy cream
1 bunch of chives, minced
3 tablespoons grated Parmesan cheese

**Preparation time** 20 minutes
**Cooking time** 50 minutes
**Level** easy
**Wine** young, fresh, sparkling red with red fruit aromas,
such as Emilia Romagna Lambrusco

Preheat the oven to 350°F.

Roll out the puff pastry and line it into an 11-inch cake pan lined with parchment paper. Pierce the dough with a fork.

Layer the ham slices over the pastry base and top with the cheese slices. Beat the eggs together with a pinch of salt, the cream, chives, and a few tablespoons of grated Parmesan. Pour the egg mixture over the cheese and bake for 50 minutes. Remove from the oven when golden brown and serve warm.

**Cook's tip** For added color and flavor, add a layer of zucchini sautéed with garlic between the ham and cheese.

# Vegetable Triangles

**Serves 4 to 6**

4 teaspoons extra-virgin olive oil
1 garlic clove
1 onion, thinly sliced
1½ cups (7 ounces) peas
9 ounces pumpkin, diced
½ cup water
1 bay leaf
1 tablespoon coriander
1 pinch ground ginger
1 teaspoon turmeric
10 sheets brek or phyllo dough
1 egg yolk, beaten
sunflower oil for frying
salt

***Preparation time*** 10 minutes
***Cooking time*** 50 minutes
***Level*** easy
***Wine*** Charmat method sparkling white with light body and a fresh grassy bouquet, such as Prosecco di Valdobbiadene Brut

Heat the olive oil in a large frying pan and add the garlic clove and onion. When the onion is soft, add the peas and pumpkin and pour in the water. Add the spices and let cook for about 30 minutes, or until the vegetables are soft. Remove from the heat, let cool, and remove and discard the bay leaf and the garlic clove.

Cut the sheets of brek or phyllo dough in half. Place 1 tablespoon of vegetable filling on each piece. Fold the pastry over into a triangle; brush with egg yolk to seal the edges and press down gently to adhere.

Heat the sunflower oil in a wide shallow pan and fry the triangles, turning over until they are evenly browned. Drain on paper towels and season with a pinch of salt. Serve immediately.

***Cook's tip*** Brek dough is a very light puff pastry found in Middle Eastern and North African cuisine.

# Pumpkin and Radicchio Pie

**Serves 6**

3 tablespoons extra-virgin olive oil
  plus extra for brushing
1 onion, thinly sliced
½ pumpkin, peeled, seeded, and diced
½ red Chioggia or Treviso radicchio, shredded
2 cups (9 ounces) peas
1 egg
salt and pepper
11 ounces pâte brisée
9 ounces puff pastry (see page 10)
  or packaged puff pastry, thawed
2 tablespoons sesame seeds
1 tablespoon sunflower seeds

**Preparation time** 25 minutes
**Cooking time** 45 minutes
**Level** easy
**Wine** well-structured white with a developed bouquet,
such as Friuli Ribolla Gialla

Preheat oven to 375°F.

Heat 1 tablespoon of the olive oil in a large frying pan and add half the onion and all of the pumpkin. Add 4 tablespoons of water and cook for 10 minutes.

Heat the remaining olive oil in another frying pan and add the remaining onion and the radicchio. Let cook for a few minutes until soft.

Meanwhile, blanch the peas in salted boiling water for 2 minutes.

Puree the pumpkin mixture in a food processor, then mix in the peas and radicchio. Add an egg and mix well to combine, then season with salt and pepper.

Line a tart tin with the pâte brisée, fill with the vegetable mixture, and cover with the puff pastry. Score the pastry surface, brush with olive oil, and dust with sesame and sunflower seeds. Bake for 30 minutes and serve warm.

# Asparagus, Carrot, and Mushroom Phyllo Roll

**Serves 4**

### Roll
1 bunch medium asparagus
3 carrots, peeled and julienned
2 medium-small fresh porcini mushrooms
6 tablespoons extra-virgin olive oil
2 garlic cloves, smashed
salt and pepper
thyme leaves
9 ounces phyllo dough

### Salad
6 fresh porcini mushrooms, thinly sliced
salt and pepper
3 tablespoons extra-virgin olive oil

**Preparation time** 25 minutes
**Cooking time** 15 minutes
**Level** easy
**Wine** young rosé with refreshing aromas of flowers and fruit,
such as Veneto Bardolino Chiaretto

Preheat oven to 425°F.

Cut off the woody bottom of the asparagus spears and steam the spears until tender.

Steam the carrots for 3 minutes.

Wipe the porcini mushrooms with a damp paper towel. Discard the earthy bottom of the stems and dice the remainder of the mushrooms. Sauté the porcini in a frying pan with a little olive oil and the garlic. Season with pinches of salt and pepper and add the thyme leaves.

Roll out 2 sheets of phyllo and place one on top of the other. Salt the dough and place the asparagus on top in parallel lines at ½-inch intervals. Fill in the spaces with the carrots, then season with salt. Drizzle with olive oil and top with the mushrooms. Carefully roll up the pastry, brush with olive oil, and sprinkle with salt.

Bake for 10 minutes.

Serve slices of the roll with a salad of the mushrooms seasoned with salt and pepper and drizzled with olive oil.

# Salmon Strudel with Fava Bean Sauce

**Serves 4**

## Strudel

7 ounces fresh salmon fillet, chopped
4 tablespoons extra-virgin olive oil
salt
chives, minced
lemon thyme, leaves
12 ounces puff pastry (see page 10),
  or packaged frozen puff pastry, thawed
melted butter

## Fava bean sauce

1 cup (3½ ounces) shelled fava beans
¼ cup (½ stick) butter
1 shallot, minced
½ dried red chili pepper, crumbled
½ cup cream

## Garnish

sunflower oil, for frying
puff pastry trimmings
balsamic vinegar

**Preparation time** 25 minutes
**Cooking time** 30 minutes
**Level** medium
**Wine** medium-bodied white with an elegant bouquet,
such as Sicily Chardonnay

Preheat oven to 375°F.

Mix the salmon with the olive oil, salt, chives, and lemon thyme. Spread the mixture on the puff pastry. Carefully roll up the pastry, brush with a little melted butter, and score the surface with a series of diagonal incisions. Transfer to a baking sheet lined with parchment paper and bake for 20 minutes.

Meanwhile, blanch the fava beans. Melt the butter in a frying pan and sauté the minced shallot and the chili pepper. Add the beans and a little warm water and cook until tender. Just before the beans are done, add the cream. Puree the mixture in a food processor and pass through a sieve.

Remove the strudel from the oven. Let cool slightly, then slice into four portions.

Heat the sunflower oil. Deep fry the puff pastry trimmings.

Serve the strudel with the cold fava sauce, puff pastry crisps, and a drizzle of balsamic vinegar.

# Chicken and Artichoke Tart

**Serves 6**

## *Pastry*
1²/₃ cups (7 ounces) all-purpose flour
1 teaspoon active dry yeast
salt and pepper
3 tablespoons extra-virgin olive oil
lukewarm water

## *Filling*
5 artichokes
juice of 1 lemon
3 tablespoons extra-virgin olive oil
1 shallot, chopped
salt and pepper
parsley or chives, chopped
11 ounces chicken breast, chopped
1 egg
2 to 3 tablespoons light cream
1 tablespoon grated Parmesan

**Preparation time** 25 minutes
**Cooking time** 35 minutes
**Level** easy
**Wine** young, light-bodied red with fresh, herbaceous aromas,
such as Alto Adige Santa Maddalena

Preheat oven to 400°F.
  Sift the flour in a bowl with the yeast, salt, and pepper. Pour in the olive oil and a little lukewarm water. Knead on a floured surface until the dough is smooth and elastic; wrap in plastic wrap and allow to rest for 1 hour.
  Remove the hard outer leaves and inner choke from each artichoke. As each is trimmed, place in a bowl of water with lemon juice. After they are all trimmed, drain and thinly slice.
  Heat the olive oil and sauté the shallot until it begins to brown. Add the artichoke slices, season with salt and pepper, and add the chopped parsley or chives. Cook until the artichokes are tender, then add the chicken and cook for 3 more minutes. Remove from the heat and let cool to room temperature.
  Beat the egg in a bowl with the cream, then add the Parmesan cheese and the chicken mixture.
  Roll out the dough and place in a high-rimmed round tart tin. Trim the overlapping dough. Pierce the base with a fork and fill with the chicken mixture. Cover the surface with dough trimmings, leaving just a small hole in the middle for the steam to vent. Bake for about 18 to 20 minutes and serve immediately.

# Potato and Bacon Tart

**Serves 6**

2 tablespoons extra-virgin olive oil
1 shallot, chopped
1 pound potatoes, peeled and sliced
2 cups hot vegetable broth
salt and pepper
3 ounces bacon, diced
1 egg, beaten
3 tablespoons grated Parmesan
9 ounces puff pastry (see page 10),
  or packaged frozen puff pastry, thawed
1 tablespoon sesame seeds

**Preparation time** 20 minutes
**Cooking time** 45 minutes
**Level** easy
**Wine** medium-bodied, young rosé with floral, fruity aromas,
such as Campania Cirò Rosato

Preheat oven to 400°F.

Heat olive oil and sauté shallot until it starts to brown. Add the potatoes and sauté. Pour in the hot broth (photo 1) and cook over medium-low heat until the potatoes are tender. Puree the mixture with an immersion blender and season to taste with salt and pepper.

Brown the bacon in a nonstick frying pan with a little olive oil until crisp. Combine the bacon with the potato puree (photo 2), then add the beaten egg (photo 3), Parmesan, and a pinch of pepper.

Line a baking dish with waxed paper, spread with the potato mixture, and cover with the puff pastry. Pierce the pastry and sprinkle with sesame seeds. Bake for about 35 minutes. Let cool slightly, then serve.

# Coppa Ham, Zucchini, and Eggplant Strudel

**Serves 4 to 6**

1 small eggplant
6 tablespoons extra-virgin olive oil
1 garlic clove
3 small zucchini
salt and pepper
5½ ounces coppa ham
9 ounces puff pastry (see page 10),
  or packaged frozen puff pastry, thawed
poppy seeds

**Preparation time** 25 minutes
**Cooking time** 35 minutes
**Level** easy
**Wine** medium-structured red with an evolving bouquet of red fruit and light spices, such as Friuli Collio Merlot

Preheat oven to 375°F.
  Cut the eggplant into wedges, remove the seeds, and dice the rest.
  Heat 5 tablespoons of the olive oil in a frying pan with the garlic and sauté the eggplant.
  Cut the zucchini into thick rounds and add to the pan. Continue cooking for a few minutes, but leave the vegetables al dente. Season with salt and pepper.
  Cut the coppa into strips and add to the vegetables. Spread the mixture onto the puff pastry sheet and close like a calzone. Brush the pastry with the remaining olive oil, then sprinkle with poppy seeds and a little salt. Bake for 25 minutes.

# Radicchio, Ham, and Asiago Strudel

**Serves 6**

### *Dough*
1¼ cups (5½ ounces) all-purpose flour
½ cup (2½ ounces) bread flour
2½ tablespoons (1 ounce) semolina flour
3 tablespoons extra-virgin olive oil
salt

### *Filling*
1 white onion, diced
4 tablespoons (2 ounces) butter
1 head of radicchio, sliced
salt and pepper
9 ounces Asiago cheese, sliced into matchsticks
5½ ounces ham, thinly sliced

*Preparation time* 25 minutes
*Cooking time* 1 hour
*Level* medium
*Wine* well-structured white with a developed bouquet of ripe fruit,
such as Campania Greco di Tufo

Mix together the flour and the semolina and add the olive oil, salt, and enough warm water to form a smooth and elastic dough. Knead until smooth, roll into a ball, and wrap in plastic wrap. Refrigerate for 1 hour.

Meanwhile, sauté the onion in half of the butter. Add the radicchio, season with salt and pepper and cook for 7 to 8 minutes.

Roll out the dough into a very thin sheet on a lightly floured surface. Cut it into a 16-inch by 20-inch rectangle and top with the radicchio mixture, the ham, and, the cheese. Roll up the dough into a strudel and carefully transfer to a baking sheet lined with wax paper. Melt the remaining butter and brush it over the top of the strudel. Bake for 45 to 50 minutes at 350°F. Cut the strudel into thick slices and serve.

*Cook's tip* If the flavor of Asiago cheese is too strong, use the same quantity of thinly sliced mozzarella instead.

# Savory Zucchini and Prosciutto Strudel

**Serves 4**

1 pound phyllo dough
7 ounces prosciutto, thinly sliced
5 small zucchini, sliced lengthwise into quarters
10 zucchini flowers
3 tablespoons extra-virgin olive oil
1 garlic clove
poppy seeds
salt

**_Preparation time_** 15 minutes
**_Cooking time_** 30 minutes
**_Level_** easy
**_Wine_** young, medium-bodied white with an elegant bouquet,
such as Sicily Etna Bianco

Preheat the oven to 350°F.
   Cut open the zucchini flowers and remove the pistils.
   Heat a little olive oil in a non-stick frying pan and brown the garlic clove. Add the zucchini and season to taste with salt. Sauté briefly and add the zucchini flowers.
   Lay out the phyllo dough. Top the dough with prosciutto and then with the zucchini mixture. Roll up the phyllo dough and brush with oil. Sprinkle with the poppy seeds and bake for 15 minutes.

# Spinach, Swiss Chard, and Ricotta Tart

**Serves 4**

1 bunch fresh spinach, or about ¾ cup cooked spinach
1 bunch fresh Swiss chard, or about ¾ cup cooked Swiss chard
1 egg
3 tablespoons grated Parmesan cheese
grated nutmeg
salt and pepper
1 cup (7 ounces) fresh ricotta
3 tablespoons extra-virgin olive oil
12 ounces puff pastry (see page 10)
  or packaged frozen puff pastry, thawed

**Preparation time** 25 minutes
**Cooking time** 45 minutes
**Level** easy
**Wine** medium-bodied, young white with a grassy bouquet,
such as Trentino Müller Thurgau

Preheat oven to 375°F.

If using fresh spinach and fresh Swiss chard, thoroughly wash each under cold running water. Cut off the spinach roots and the white chard stalks. Wash again and blanch in salted boiling water for about 5 minutes. Drain and set aside to cool.

Coarsely chop the spinach and Swiss chard and place in a bowl. Add the egg, Parmesan, and nutmeg and season with salt and pepper. Fold in the ricotta and olive oil, adding a pinch of salt if necessary.

Roll the puff pastry out on a floured work surface. Lightly flour a round tart tin (8 inches in diameter) and line it with the pastry, leaving a border. Pierce the pastry crust with a fork and pour in the filling. Fold the edges of the pastry toward the middle and bake for about 25 minutes. Remove the tart from the oven and let cool before serving.

# Tuna and Broccoli Pie

## TUNA

Preserved tuna is one of the world's most popular fish products. There are several varieties of tuna, in oil and brine, and different levels of quality. The best is made using the freshest fish. Once canned tuna is opened it should be transferred to a jar or glass container.

**Serves 6**

### *Pâte brisée*
2 ½ cups (11 ounces) all-purpose flour
salt
¾ cup (1 ½ sticks) butter, softened and chopped
¾ cup cold water

### *Filling*
4 slices of sandwich bread, diced
¾ cup milk
1 head of broccoli, cut into florets
3 tablespoons extra-virgin olive oil
1 garlic clove, smashed
½ chili pepper, seeded and minced
salt and pepper
1 cup (7 ounces) tuna in oil, drained
2 tablespoons capers
parsley
1 red onion, thinly sliced

*Preparation time* 20 minutes
*Cooking time* 40 minutes
*Level* easy
*Wine* well-structured white with a developed bouquet of ripe fruit, such as Sicily Bianco d'Alcamo

Preheat oven to 400°F.

Mound the flour on a work surface, add a pinch of salt, and make a well in the center. Add the butter and slowly pour in the cold water. Knead until the dough is white and smooth. Wrap in plastic wrap and let rest in the refrigerator for 20 minutes. Soak the bread in the milk.

Blanch the broccoli florets in salted boiling water for 3 minutes. Drain.

Heat the olive oil in a frying pan and sauté the garlic, chili pepper, and blanched broccoli florets over high heat for a few minutes. Remove from heat, season to taste with salt, and transfer to a bowl.

Drain the bread and squeeze out the excess milk. Puree the tuna, capers, bread, and parsley in a food processor. Combine the puree with the broccoli and season to taste with salt and pepper.

Roll the pâte brisée out on a floured work surface. Flour an aluminum tart tin and line it with the pastry. Pierce the base with a fork and fill with the broccoli mixture.

Sprinkle the onion slices over the top of the tart. Season with a drizzle of olive oil and bake for 30 to 35 minutes.

# Squash Tart

**Serves 6 to 8**

3 zucchini, trimmed
1 white onion, finely chopped
2 tablespoons extra-virgin olive oil
2 tablespoons butter
2 carrots, peeled and diced
¼ round, green-skinned pumpkin,
  peeled, seeded, and diced
salt and pepper
2 cups hot vegetable broth
14 ounces pâte brisée (see page 74)
1 egg
thyme, chopped
¼ cup pumpkin seeds

**Preparation time** 25 minutes
**Cooking time** 50 minutes
**Level** easy
**Wine** medium-bodied, young, fresh and fragrant white,
such as Veneto Lugana

Preheat oven to 375°F.
   Slice the zucchini lengthwise into quarters and cut out the seedy white center. Dice the green part and set aside.
   Sauté the onion in a frying pan with the olive oil and butter, add the carrots, and then add the pumpkin. Season with pinches of salt and pepper. Pour in the hot broth, cover, and cook for 7 minutes. Add the zucchini and cook until tender. Remove from heat and let cool.
   Roll the pâte brisée out on a floured work surface to ¼-inch thickness. Line a floured tart tin with the dough and pierce the base with a fork. Mix the egg and thyme with the vegetable filling and pour into the pastry. Sprinkle with the pumpkin seeds and bake for about 40 minutes.

# Sesame Tart with Eggplant and Zucchini

**Serves 6**

### *Pastry*
2 tablespoons sesame seeds
1³/₄ cups all-purpose flour
½ teaspoon active dry yeast
salt
1 tablespoon sesame oil
lukewarm water

### *Filling*
1 large or 2 small eggplants
4 large zucchini
2 spring onions, chopped
3 tablespoons extra-virgin olive oil
salt and pepper
lemon thyme, chopped
½ cup warm vegetable broth or water
1 egg white, lightly beaten
2 tablespoons grated Parmesan

**Preparation time** 20 minutes
**Cooking time** 50 minutes
**Level** easy
**Wine** well-structured white with an intense and aromatic bouquet,
such as Friuli Collio Sauvignon

Preheat oven to 400°F.

Toast the sesame seeds in a nonstick pan until well browned.

Place the flour into a bowl, then add the yeast, salt, sesame oil, and toasted sesame seeds. Mix in enough lukewarm water to form a thick dough, and knead until smooth. Wrap the dough in plastic wrap and refrigerate.

Cut the eggplant into 8 segments, remove and discard the white, seedy center, and dice the rest. Slice the zucchini into thin rounds.

Brown the spring onions in a frying pan with the olive oil over low heat and add the eggplant. Cover and cook for 5 to 6 minutes, adding a pinch of salt. Add the zucchini and lemon thyme and sauté briefly. Pour in the warm broth or water. Cook until vegetables are just tender, then puree in a blender or food processor. Let cool slightly, and then add the egg white with a little salt and the Parmesan. Season with salt and pepper.

Roll out the dough and line a floured tart tin; prick the base with a fork and fill with the vegetable sauce. Bake for 35 minutes. Serve the tart at room temperature or cold.

# Trout Parcels

**Serves 4**

### *Pastry*
½ cup water
½ cup extra-virgin olive oil
salt
4 cups (1 pound, 2 ounces) all-purpose flour

### *Filling*
1 small cauliflower, cut into florets
¼ cup white wine
2 cups (7 ounces) shredded savoy cabbage
6 tablespoons extra-virgin olive oil
1 garlic clove, crushed
salt and white pepper
11 ounces trout fillet
3 shallots, chopped
1 parsley sprig, chopped
1 egg, beaten

**Preparation time** 40 minutes
**Cooking time** 30 minutes
**Level** medium
**Wine** young, medium-bodied white with a fresh and grassy bouquet,
such as Alto Adige Pinot Bianco

Preheat oven to 400°F.

Mix the water, olive oil, and a pinch of salt together with the flour to form an elastic dough. Wrap in plastic wrap and let rest in the refrigerator.

Blanch the cauliflower florets in salted boiling water with the wine for 5 minutes. Drain and transfer to an ice bath. When cooled, drain and pat dry.

Sauté the savoy cabbage with the olive oil and garlic. Season with pinches of salt and white pepper then set aside.

Remove the skin and any bones from the trout fillet, and dice.

Cook the shallot over low heat in a frying pan with a little water and the parsley until soft.

Using a rolling pin, roll out the dough to a ¼-inch

thickness. Cut the dough into 2-inch squares. Place a teaspoon of cabbage, a few pieces of trout, and 1 cauliflower floret in the center of each square. Top with a teaspoon of chopped shallots and fold up the corners of the dough squares to form little parcels. Brush the parcels with the beaten egg and bake for 20 minutes. Serve hot.

# Focaccia

This chapter presents a variety of thin and crispy flatbreads flavored with simple and tasty ingredients. Thanks to these easy and quick recipes, you'll be able to prepare light and original meals, as well as snacks to nibble on with drinks.

# Onion and Black Olive Focaccia

**Serves 4**

### Dough
4 teaspoons active dry yeast
½ teaspoon honey
4 cups (1 pound, 2 ounces) all-purpose
  flour
salt
2 tablespoons extra-virgin olive oil

### Topping
2 tablespoons extra-virgin olive oil
3 medium onions, sliced
2 tablespoons black olives, pitted
marjoram and oregano

**Preparation time** 15 minutes
**Cooking time** 35 minutes
**Level** easy
**Beer** Italian Lager

### ONIONS
Five thousand years ago, onions were already being cultivated in some parts of northern Asia and in Palestine. They were much appreciated by both the ancient Egyptians and Greeks, and during the Peloponnesian wars, onions were regarded as the supreme food for the army.

Dissolve the yeast in lukewarm water and the honey. Let sit for about 10 minutes.

Mix the flour with salt and olive oil and add the yeast mixture. Knead well and let rest for 3 hours.

Preheat oven to 300°F.

Heat the olive oil for the topping in a frying pan and sauté the onions with 2 tablespoons of water until translucent. Add the olives, oregano, and marjoram.

Stretch or roll the dough out in an oiled baking sheet. Sprinkle with the onion mixture and bake for 25 minutes. Serve hot.

**Cook's tip** To make the onions less pungent, slice them into rings, then microwave them on high for 1 minute before sautéing.

# Corn Focaccia with Pancetta

**Serves 4**

1 pound, 9 ounces focaccia dough (see page 10)
5½ ounces pancetta or bacon, diced
¼ cup cornmeal
3 tablespoons extra-virgin olive oil
salt and pepper
1 bunch aromatic herbs (rosemary, sage, thyme, chives), chopped

**Preparation time** 20 minutes
**Cooking time** 25 minutes
**Level** easy
**Beer** English Bitter Ale

Let the dough rise until doubled in volume, then knead vigorously, adding 2 tablespoons of the diced bacon and a sprinkle of cornmeal.

Roll out the dough on a baking sheet, leaving it rather thick. Brush with the extra-virgin olive oil and dust with cornmeal.

Preheat oven to 400°F.

Fill a spray bottle with water and spray the focaccia lightly to dampen its surface. Lightly season with salt and pepper, and let rise in a warm place for about 20 minutes.

Bake the focaccia for 25 minutes. Halfway through, sprinkle with the herbs and remaining bacon.

Remove from oven and cut into slices. Serve with a plate of cooked vegetables, if desired.

# Tomato and Oregano Flatbread

**Serves 4**

1 pound, 9 ounces focaccia dough (see page 10)
4 tablespoons extra-virgin olive oil
salt and pepper
2 tomatoes, thinly sliced
1 teaspoon dried oregano

**Preparation time** 25 minutes
**Cooking time** 20 minutes
**Level** easy
**Beer** Czech Pilsner

Knead the dough, then roll it out on a floured work surface. Lightly oil a baking sheet and then line it with the dough. Dust with a little salt and pepper, brush with olive oil, and let rise in a warm place for 25 minutes.

Preheat oven to 450°F.

Arrange the tomatoes on the surface of the dough, leaving about ½ inch between the slices. Sprinkle with the oregano and a pinch of salt.

Bake for about 20 minutes. Let cool slightly, then cut into slices. Serve as a tasty afternoon snack.

**Cook's tip** For a richer version of this focaccia, replace the fresh tomatoes with sun-dried San Marzano tomatoes marinated in oil.

# Rosemary Crackers

**SUNFLOWER OIL**
Sunflower oil is good not only for frying, but also for use in recipes requiring an oil that is neutral in taste. A very delicate extra-virgin olive oil may be used in place of sunflower oil in the latter instance.

**Serves 4 to 6**

1 cup plus 3 tablespoons
 (5⅓ ounces) all-purpose flour
4 tablespoons sunflower oil
2 tablespoons extra-virgin olive oil
2 rosemary sprigs, leaves only,
 chopped
4 tablespoons lukewarm water
sea salt flakes

**Preparation time** 20 minutes
**Cooking time** 4 minutes
**Level** easy
**Beer** Italian Lager

Place the flour in a bowl and add the sunflower oil, olive oil, and half the rosemary. Pour in the water and mix with fingertips until combined.

Transfer the dough to a work surface and knead vigorously with the palms of your hands, adding some flour if the dough seems too soft and wet. Continue kneading until it forms a smooth and elastic ball, then wrap in plastic wrap and refrigerate for about 20 minutes.

Preheat oven to 480°F.

Divide the dough into small portions and roll them out thinly, one at a time, using a pasta machine (or a rolling pin, taking care to flour the work surface well).

Lay the strips on a baking tray and sprinkle with the remaining rosemary and the sea salt. Bake for about 4 minutes. Remove from the oven and let cool.

**Cook's tip** Once the strips are baked and cooled, break them into smaller pieces to create bite-size crackers to accompany a meal or to enjoy as a snack.

# Green Olive and Bell Pepper Focaccia

**Serves 4**

1 red bell pepper
20 green olives, pitted
1 pound, 9 ounces focaccia dough (see page 10)
3 tablespoons extra-virgin olive oil plus extra for oiling baking sheet
1 garlic clove
salt

**Preparation time** 20 minutes
**Cooking time** 30 minutes
**Level** easy
**Beer** German Pilsner

Halve the bell pepper, remove the white pith and seeds, and cut the flesh into small strips.

Drain the olives from any brine or oil, and pat dry with a paper towel.

Let the dough rise until doubled in volume, then roll out and use to line an oiled baking sheet. Spread the olives over the surface of the dough. Let rise again in a warm place for 20 minutes.

Preheat oven to 425°F.

Meanwhile, heat the olive oil in a frying pan and sauté the garlic clove. Add the pepper strips and sauté over high heat for 7 to 8 minutes. Remove from heat and pour off any excess oil, then spread the peppers over the focaccia. Sprinkle with a pinch of salt and bake for about 18 minutes.

Remove from oven, then take the focaccia off the baking sheet and cut into rectangular slices.

**Cook's tip** If you want to make this dish even more quickly, toss the raw pepper strips with olive oil, salt, pepper, and a little thyme, then spread them directly on the dough so they cook in the oven.

# Onion, Anchovy, and Caper Focaccia

**Serves 4**

2 small white onions, thinly sliced into rings
3 tablespoons extra-virgin olive oil
1 pound, 9 ounces focaccia dough (see page 10)
1 tablespoon capers, drained, rinsed, and roughly chopped
10 anchovy fillets in oil, drained and roughly chopped
salt and pepper

**Preparation time** 20 minutes
**Cooking time** 18 minutes
**Level** easy
**Beer** Irish Stout

Soak the onions in a bowl of cold water to make them less pungent.

Oil a baking sheet and line it with the dough, rolling the dough out with a rolling pin, then pushing it out with your fingertips.

Preheat oven to 425°F.

Drain the onions, dry them with paper towels, then spread the onions over the surface of the dough. Cover with a damp kitchen towel and let rise in a warm place for 20 minutes.

Sprinkle the focaccia with capers, anchovies, and the remaining olive oil, then bake for 18 minutes. Remove from the oven, let cool, season with salt and pepper to taste, then cut into small pieces before serving.

# Saffron Focaccia with Zucchini

**Serves 4**

½ teaspoon saffron
1 tablespoon water
1 pound, 9 ounces focaccia dough (see page 10)
3 baby zucchini
3 tablespoons extra-virgin olive oil
salt and black pepper

**Preparation time** 20 minutes
**Cooking time** 15 minutes
**Level** easy
**Beer** German Weizen

Dissolve the saffron in 1 tablespoon of water, then mix it into the dough. Stretch or roll out the dough until thin, then lay it on a lightly oiled baking sheet. Let rise in a warm place.

Preheat oven to 425°F.

Meanwhile, trim and thinly slice the zucchini, using a mandoline or a very sharp knife.

Brush the surface of the dough with olive oil, sprinkle with salt, and cover with the zucchini so that the slices overlap slightly. Sprinkle with some more salt and pepper.

Bake for about 17 to 18 minutes, until the edges are golden brown. Let cool, then cut into squares and serve.

**Cook's tip** Whole saffron pistils can also be mixed into the dough so that they are visible in the focaccia. Adding some thyme leaves will make the focaccia even more flavorful.

# Savory Apple Focaccia

**Serves 6**

3 1/3 cups (1 pound) all-purpose flour
3/4 cup plus 1 tablespoon water
4 1/2 teaspoons yeast
salt
3 tablespoons extra-virgin olive oil
1 1/2 tablespoons minced shallot
1 apple, diced
1 teaspoon confectioners' sugar
1 teaspoon marjoram

**Preparation time** 15 minutes
**Cooking time** 30 minutes
**Level** easy
**Beer** Belgian White Beer

Mix the flour with the water, yeast, and a pinch of salt. Knead the dough vigorously, then allow to rest for about 15 minutes.

Heat the olive oil in a frying pan and sauté the shallot and apple with the confectioners' sugar and marjoram. Knead the mixture into the dough and let rest for 2 hours, until doubled in volume.

Preheat oven to 365°F.

Roll the dough and place on a baking sheet. Bake for 17 minutes, then reduce the oven temperature to 300°F and continue baking for another 13 minutes.

Serve the focaccia warm, paired with a selection of cured meats.

# Beyond Sandwiches

Turn the page to discover recipes for
stuffed piadina, sandwiches, and
croquettes that are sure to please.
You'll find all sorts of options that will
enable you to turn a quick lunch
or a simple snack with friends into
a moment of pure pleasure.

# Asparagus Fritters

**Serves 4**

6 thin asparagus spears
11 ounces panzerotto dough (see page 13)
salt and freshly ground black pepper
1 thyme sprig
sunflower oil for frying

**Preparation time** 10 minutes
**Cooking time** 10 minutes
**Level** easy
**Wine** Charmat method sparkling white with light body and fresh flavors,
such as Prosecco di Valdobbiadene Extra Dry

Snap off the hard base of the asparagus spears, and peel the lower half of each
remaining spear with a vegetable peeler. Blanch the asparagus in salted boiling water
for about 3 minutes, then drain and immerse in cold water. Once cooled, thinly slice
into rounds.

Knead the dough and mix in a pinch of pepper, the thyme leaves, and the asparagus
until evenly incorporated.

Heat the sunflower oil and fry spoonfuls of the dough. Drain on paper towels,
sprinkle with salt, and serve immediately.

**Cook's tip** For lighter fritters, replace the classic panzerotto dough with a thick batter
made from flour and cold sparkling water.

# Rustic Sandwiches with Stracchino and Salami

**Serves 4**

4½ ounces fresh stracchino, crescenza, or Taleggio cheese
1 tablespoon extra-virgin olive oil
4 thick slices of country-style bread
freshly ground black pepper
5 ounces finocchiona salami, soppressata, or other Italian salami, sliced

***Preparation time*** 10 minutes
***Cooking time*** none
***Level*** easy
***Wine*** young, light-bodied and softly structured red,
such as Morellino di Scansano

Beat the cheese with the olive oil until smooth and creamy, then spread on the slices of bread. Sprinkle with black pepper. Top two slices of bread with the salami, then cover with the other two slices. Press down gently, then cut the sandwiches in half. Serve with a glass of good red wine.

***Cook's tip*** Finocchiona, also known as *sbriciolona*, is a Tuscan salami with a crumbly texture. It is made with fennel seeds, which give it a distinctive taste and help preserve the meat. Fennel was often used as a preservative in the past, when pepper was rare and expensive.

# Crispy Piadina with Crab Salad

**Serves 4**

4 piadina (see page 13)
7 ounces crab meat
3 tablespoons extra-virgin olive oil
salt and pepper
parsley, chopped
juice of ½ lemon
1 head of green lettuce (iceberg or curly leaf), shredded
5 ounces grilled eggplant in oil, drained and patted dry
10 cherry tomatoes, quartered

**Preparation time** 20 minutes
**Cooking time** 10 minutes
**Level** easy
**Wine** medium-bodied, young white with a rich and aromatic bouquet,
such as Trebbiano di Romagna

Preheat oven to 350°F.
   Bake the piadina for 7 minutes, or until crispy.
   Meanwhile, drain the crab meat and mix with olive oil, salt, pepper, and parsley. Add the lemon juice. Toss the shredded lettuce with the mixture. Add the eggplant and tomatoes, and season to taste with olive oil and salt.
   Serve the salad on top of the piadina.

# Calabrian Mozzarella Parcels

**Serves 4**

3½ ounces sun-dried San Marzano tomatoes
1 tablespoon salted capers
5 ounces mozzarella, diced
oregano
11 ounces panzerotto dough (see page 13)
sunflower oil for frying
salt

**Preparation time** 15 minutes
**Cooking time** 5 minutes
**Level** easy
**Wine** well-structured white with an evolved bouquet of ripe fruit,
such as Calabria Cirò Bianco

Cover the sun-dried tomatoes with lukewarm water and let soak for 1 hour. Drain and dry, then roughly chop.

Rinse the capers, changing the water at least 3 times. Drain and chop roughly. Mix the tomatoes, mozzarella, and capers in a bowl with the oregano.

Roll out the dough on a floured work surface. Cut into small squares. Place a spoonful of filling in the center of each square, then fold in the edges, pressing gently to seal the dough together.

Heat the sunflower oil, then fry the parcels until golden. Drain and dry on paper towels. Sprinkle with salt and serve immediately.

**Cook's tip** For even more flavor, use sun-dried tomatoes that have been marinated in a mix of olive oil, garlic, chili pepper, and oregano.

# Piadina with Mozzarella, Tomatoes, and Prosciutto

## PROSCIUTTO

Prosciutto is a cured ham. There are a number of different varieties, with the most famous coming from Parma, San Daniele, and Norcia. Differences in taste come mainly from the different microclimates in which the prosciutto is aged. For this reason, each type of prosciutto is produced exclusively in a limited geographical area.

**Serves 4**

3 tomatoes, thickly sliced
salt
1 pinch oregano
4 warm piadina (see page 13)
11 ounces buffalo mozzarella, thinly sliced
3½ ounces prosciutto, thinly sliced
2 tablespoons extra-virgin olive oil
1 bunch basil

**Preparation time** 15 minutes
**Cooking time** 5 minutes
**Level** easy
**Wine** Charmat method sparkling white with fresh flavors and light body, such as Prosecco di Valdobbiadene Brut

Heat a cast-iron grill pan and grill the tomato slices for 1 minute on each side. Sprinkle with salt and oregano.

Fill the warm piadina with the mozzarella, prosciutto, and tomato. Season with salt and the olive oil, and add the basil leaves. Fold over and serve immediately.

**Cook's tip** The contrast between the warm grilled tomatoes, fresh mozzarella, and salty prosciutto gives this dish its appeal.

# Ricotta and Olive Wraps

**Serves 4**

### Wraps
3 San Marzano tomatoes, seeded and diced
1 thyme sprig, chopped
salt and pepper
2 tablespoons extra-virgin olive oil
½ cup (2 ounces) pitted black olives or tapenade
1 cup (9 ounces) ricotta
4 piadina (see page 13)

### Garnish
1 bunch arugula
black olive tapenade

**Preparation time** 15 minutes
**Level** easy
**Wine** young, medium-bodied white with an intense bouquet,
such as Friuli Pinot Grigio

Toss the diced tomatoes with thyme, salt, pepper, and a drizzle of olive oil. Let sit for 10 minutes to allow flavors to combine, then drain off excess liquid.

If using whole olives, place them in a food processor with the ricotta and a pinch of salt, and puree until smooth. If using a tapenade, mix in a bowl with the ricotta and salt to taste.

Spread the ricotta-olive mixture over the piadina, leaving ¾ inch around the edges. Sprinkle with the tomatoes. Roll up piadina and let sit for 10 minutes.

Cut into slices on the diagonal and serve on a bed of arugula with tapenade.

# Mini Focaccias with Tapenade and Prosciutto

**Serves 4**

1 pound pre-risen pizza dough
4 tablespoons extra-virgin olive oil
3 tablespoons milk
3 ½ ounces green olive tapenade
7 ounces prosciutto, thinly sliced

**Preparation time** 20 minutes
**Cooking time** 10 minutes
**Level** easy
**Wine** young, sparkling red with fresh, fruity flavors,
such as Emilia Romagna Lambrusco

Roll out the dough and cut it into circles about 3 to 4 inches in diameter. Arrange them on an oiled baking sheet. Let them rise for 20 minutes in a warm place.

Preheat the oven to 425°F.

Mix together the milk and 2 tablespoons olive oil. Brush the foccacias with the mixture. Bake for 10 minutes. Remove from the oven and cover with a clean kitchen towel. Let cool.

Halve the foccacias and fill them with the tapenade and the prosciutto. Close and serve.

**Cook's tip** The tapenade can be replaced by artichoke or asparagus pâté.

# Mini Bell Pepper and Mushroom Tarts

**Serves 4**

½ red bell pepper
½ yellow bell pepper
½ green bell pepper
3 porcini mushrooms
3 tablespoons extra-virgin olive oil
salt and pepper
9 ounces puff pastry (see page 10)
  or packaged frozen puff pastry, thawed
thyme leaves

**Preparation time** 20 minutes
**Cooking time** 20 minutes
**Level** easy
**Wine** light-bodied, young red with a soft structure,
such as Veneto Piave Merlot

Preheat oven to 400°F.
   Seed the peppers and remove the white membranes. Finely dice the flesh
(photo 1).
   Peel the mushrooms and chop off and discard the earthy part of the stalk. Thinly
slice the mushrooms.
   Heat the olive oil in a frying pan and sauté the peppers. Add the mushrooms
(photo 2) and cook for a few more minutes. Season to taste with salt and pepper.
   Roll out the puff pastry and cut into rounds using a fluted cookie cutter. Top
with spoonfuls of the pepper-mushroom mixture (photo 3). Sprinkle with thyme
and bake for about 15 minutes. Serve warm as a tasty appetizer.

# Bread

Welcome to the world of loaves, rolls, and breadsticks, all of which will bring that freshly baked aroma into your kitchen. Thanks to original recipes that are sure to surprise and delight, you can make this most basic of foods the star of your table.

# Mediterranean Bread

**Makes 5 loaves**

### First dough
2 cups (9 ounces) all-purpose flour
½ cup plus 1½ teaspoon lukewarm water
4 teaspoons active dry yeast

### Second dough
2 cups (9 ounces) all-purpose flour plus extra for dusting
½ cup plus 1 tablespoon lukewarm water
3 tablespoons extra-virgin olive oil plus extra for oiling salt

**Preparation time** 40 minutes
**Cooking time** 30 minutes
**Level** medium

Mix together the flour, lukewarm water, and yeast for the first dough. Knead, then let rise at room temperature, covered with a clean kitchen towel, for about 3 hours.

Mix the flour for the second dough, 7 tablespoons of the lukewarm water, and the extra-virgin olive oil into the first dough. Dissolve a pinch of salt in the remaining lukewarm water, pour it over the dough, and continue kneading. Place the dough in a lightly oiled bowl and let rise for about 20 minutes. Stretch or roll out the dough on a work surface and brush with olive oil. Fold it in half 4 times and let sit for 20 minutes.

Divide the dough into small portions (photo 1), then shape them into rolls (photos 2 and 3). Arrange the rolls on a baking sheet, brush with olive oil, and dust with flour. Let rise again for 1 hour 10 minutes in a warm, draft-free place. Preheat oven to 475°F. Bake the rolls for 30 minutes or until well browned.

**Cook's tip** Making bread at home is not as hard as it might seem. You just need to know the right process and use the best ingredients. Most important is the yeast. Natural leavening is used by professional bakers. Baking powder can be used for quick breads and muffins, which rise during the baking. Active dry yeast is most popular for home baking.

1      2      3

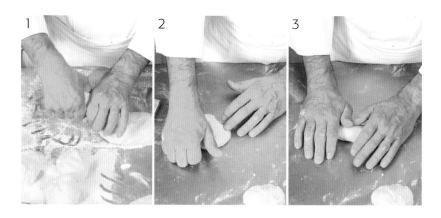

# Giant Breadsticks

**Makes 35 breadsticks**

### *First dough*
1 cup (5 ounces) semolina flour plus extra for dusting
7 tablespoons water
4 teaspoons active dry yeast

### *Second dough*
1½ cups plus 4½ teaspoons (7 ounces) all-purpose flour
¼ cup (1¾ ounces) malt flour
2 tablespoons lard
1 tablespoon active dry yeast
½ cup plus 2 tablespoons extra-virgin olive oil
salt
½ cup water
1 teaspoon malt extract

**Preparation time** 20 minutes
**Cooking time** 15 minutes
**Level** medium

Put the semolina flour, water, and yeast for the first dough in a food processor and mix until it forms a smooth ball. Place in a bowl, cover with plastic wrap, and let rise for at least 1½ hours.

Mound the all-purpose flour and malt flour for the second dough on a work surface and place the first dough in the center. Add the lard, yeast, ½ cup olive oil, a pinch of salt, water, and malt extract. Mix all of the ingredients together and knead vigorously to obtain a soft, smooth dough. Roll the dough out slightly, then fold it up and form into a roll about 2 to 2½ inches thick. Brush with the remaining olive oil and let rest for 1 hour.

Preheat oven to 400°F, with a small saucepan of water on the lowest rack.

Transfer the roll of dough to a work surface dusted with semolina flour. Using a spatula, cut the dough into small sticks about ¾ inch thick. Dust again with more semolina flour. Take one piece at a time and stretch it out to a thick stick, about 7 inches long. Arrange the sticks on a baking sheet lined with waxed paper and let rise for about 20 minutes. Bake for 15 minutes.

# Baguettes

**Makes 5 baguettes**

### First dough
6¼ cups plus 2½ tablespoons (1 pound, 12 ounces) all-purpose flour
2 cups lukewarm water
2 tablespoons active dry yeast

### Second dough
2⅓ cups (10½ ounces) all-purpose flour
⅔ cup water
1½ teaspoon active dry yeast
1 tablespoon salt

**Preparation time** 50 minutes
**Cooking time** 30 minutes
**Level** medium

Mix the ingredients for the first dough until they come together, forming a ball. Leave the dough to rise in a warm place for about 3 hours. The dough should triple in volume.

Once the dough is ready, mix in the flour, water, yeast, and salt for the second dough. Knead for 10 to 12 minutes, until smooth and elastic. Let rise for about 30 minutes.

Shape the dough into small balls, each weighing a little more than an ounce. Knead each ball individually, then let rise for 20 minutes. Create baguettes, elongating each ball by rolling first in the center and then moving toward the ends to prevent air bubbles from appearing on the surface. Leave the baguettes to rise until increased in volume but still firm.

Preheat oven to 400°F.

Make 3 to 4 diagonal cuts on the top of each baguette, then bake for about 25 to 30 minutes.

**Cook's tip** For a shinier crust, brush the surface of the baguettes with an egg white wash before baking.

# Multi-Grain Bread

**Makes 3 loaves**

### First dough
4 cups (1 pound, 2 ounces) all-purpose flour
1 cup water
4½ teaspoons active dry yeast

### Second dough
6 tablespoons plus 1½ teaspoons all-purpose flour
2 tablespoons rye flour
2 tablespoons spelt flour
2 tablespoons buckwheat flour
2 tablespoons fine cornmeal
½ cup plus 1 tablespoon water
1 teaspoon active dry yeast
salt
4 tablespoons oats

**Preparation time** 45 minutes
**Cooking time** 30 minutes
**Level** medium

Mix together the ingredients for the first dough until they come together and form a ball, then let rise, covered with a kitchen towel, for about 3 hours.

Sift all the flours and the cornmeal for the second dough and mix them into the first dough with the water and yeast. Knead thoroughly to obtain a firm, elastic dough, then knead in a pinch of salt and the oats. Let the dough rise for about 40 to 50 minutes. Cut the dough into 3 pieces and roll them out into loaves (photo 1). Let them rest a few minutes, then place them in small floured bannetons, or bentwood shaping baskets (photo 2). Let rise in a warm place for about 1 hour, until the dough has doubled in volume and taken on the shape of the basket. Preheat oven to 425°F.

Carefully invert the loaves out of their baskets and onto a baking sheet. Score the surface of the dough lengthwise. Bake until browned and cooked through.

# Turin-Style Breadsticks

## Makes 40 thin breadsticks (grissini)

1 teaspoon active dry yeast
1 cup lukewarm water
4 cups (1 pound, 2 ounces) all-purpose flour
1 tablespoon butter, melted and cooled
salt
extra-virgin olive oil

**Preparation time** 30 minutes
**Cooking time** 15 minutes
**Level** medium

Dissolve the yeast in the lukewarm water and mix with the flour; add the butter and a pinch of salt. Work the dough into a ball, then shape into rolls and let rest on a floured work surface for 15 minutes.

Slightly flatten the rolls and brush with olive oil. Cover with plastic wrap and a kitchen towel. When the rolls are slightly puffed up, oil them again, press down, and let rise for 1 hour.

The rolls will be quite thick, like bananas. Cut them into small pieces and stretch them into thick strings by hand on a floured work surface. Arrange them on a baking tray and let rise for 15 minutes.

Preheat oven to 450°F. Bake for 12 to 15 minutes.

**Cook's tip** These thin and crispy breadsticks are generally served as a snack with finely sliced salami, as an accompaniment for a rich, creamy vegetable soup, or as a companion to mixed vegetable salads with lettuce, cucumbers, or tomatoes.

# Bell Pepper Rolls

## Makes 10 rolls

### First dough
¾ cup (3½ ounces) all-purpose flour
3 tablespoons water
1 teaspoon active dry yeast

### Second dough
2⅓ cups (10½ ounces) all-purpose flour
⅓ cup water
1 tablespoon active dry yeast
salt
1 pinch chopped parsley
1 cup (8½ ounces) diced red bell pepper
rye flour for dusting

**Preparation time** 50 minutes
**Cooking time** 20 minutes
**Level** medium

Prepare the first dough by mixing the flour, water, and yeast. Let rise in a warm place, covered with a cloth, for about 3 hours.

Knead the second dough's flour, water, and yeast into the first dough, also kneading in the salt and parsley. When the dough is smooth, knead in the diced pepper. Let rest for 1 hour.

Preheat oven to 450°F.

Cut the dough into small pieces and roll them into balls. Arrange on a baking sheet and dust with rye flour. Bake for 20 minutes, until evenly browned.

# Pumpkin Bread

**Makes 2 loaves**

### First dough
¾ cup (3½ ounces) all-purpose flour
1 teaspoon active dry yeast
water

### Second dough
4 cups (1 pound plus 1⅔ ounces) all-purpose flour
10 ounces pumpkin, roasted and mashed
7 tablespoons water
¼ cup sugar
1½ tablespoon butter
2 teaspoons salt
2 tablespoons active dry yeast


**Preparation time** 50 minutes
**Cooking time** 25 minutes
**Level** medium


Prepare the first dough, mixing the flour and yeast with enough water to form a smooth dough. Let rise at room temperature for about 3 hours.

Knead the rest of the ingredients into the first dough. Allow to rest for about 40 minutes.

Cut the dough into two pieces. Shape them into loaves as desired. Let rise at room temperature in a warm, draft-free place for 45 to 50 minutes.

Preheat oven to 450°F. Bake the rolls for about 25 minutes.

# Sunflower Seed Bread

**Makes 3 loaves**

### First dough
¾ cup (3½ ounces) all-purpose flour
¼ cup water
1 teaspoon active dry yeast

### Second dough
1 cup (5½ ounces) sunflower seeds
1½ cups plus 4½ teaspoons (7 ounces) all-purpose flour
¾ cup (3½ ounces) rye flour, plus extra for dusting
¾ cup plus 1 tablespoon water
1 tablespoon active dry yeast
1 pinch salt

**Preparation time** 45 minutes
**Cooking time** 40 minutes
**Level** medium

To prepare the first dough, mix the flour, water, and yeast and let rise under a cloth at room temperature for 3 hours.

Toast the sunflower seeds briefly in a nonstick frying pan.

Knead all of the ingredients required for the second dough, except the sunflower seeds and salt, with the first dough. Add the salt halfway through kneading, and add the sunflower seeds at the end. Knead for a few more minutes, then let rise for 40 to 50 minutes.

Cut the dough into equal numbers of large and small pieces and roll them into balls. Let rest for 10 to 15 minutes.

Place the large balls on a baking sheet and use a rolling pin to make a cross in the surface (photo 1). Place a small ball in the center of each cross (photo 2). Lightly dust with rye flour and let rise under a cloth in a warm, draft-free place for 50 to 60 minutes. Preheat oven to 425°F.

Bake the rolls for 40 minutes, until golden brown.

1  2

# Sesame and Pepper Breadsticks

## Makes about 35 thin breadsticks

### First dough

1 cup (5 ounces) semolina flour
7 tablespoons water
4½ teaspoons (1 ounce) active dry yeast
1 tablespoon sugar

### Second dough

3 tablespoons (1 ounce) sesame seeds
1⅔ cups (7 ounces) all-purpose flour
⅓ cup (1½ ounces) barley malt flour
3 tablespoons (1½ ounces) melted butter
2 teaspoons (⅓ ounce) active dry yeast
6 tablespoons extra-virgin olive oil
2 teaspoons salt
black pepper
½ cup water

### Additional

2 tablespoons extra-virgin olive oil
semolina flour
4 tablespoons sesame seeds

**Preparation time** 30 minutes
**Cooking time** 15 minutes
**Level** medium

Combine the ingredients for the first dough in an electric mixer and mix to form a smooth, elastic dough. Place the dough in a large bowl, cover with plastic wrap, and let rise for at least 1½ hours.

Meanwhile, toast the sesame seeds for the second dough and grind them into a coarse meal in a food processor. Sift the two flours for the second dough and mound them onto a work surface. Make a well in the center. Place the risen first dough and the ground sesame seeds in the center. Add the butter, yeast, olive oil, salt, pepper, and water. Knead vigorously until the dough becomes a smooth and uniform ball. Roll out the dough to form a rectangle 2 to 2½ inches thick. Brush the dough with 2 tablespoons olive oil and let rise for 1 hour, or until doubled in size. Preheat oven to 400°F. Place a baking dish filled with water in the bottom of oven. Sprinkle a work surface with semolina flour and lay the dough on top. Cut the dough into 1-inch thick strips. Using your fingertips, gently hold the ends of each strip and pull into thin sticks about 8 inches long. Roll the breadsticks in the 4 tablespoons of sesame seeds and place on a baking sheet lined with parchment paper. Let the thin breadsticks rise for another 40 minutes and then bake for 15 minutes.

# Chefs' Tools

FEATURING INNOVATIVE AND SPECIALIZED DESIGNS, HERE ARE SOME UTENSILS THAT WILL BE HELPFUL FOR PIZZA COOKS.

1 **Extendable baking sheet** This highly useful nonstick baking sheet can stretch from 13 to 21 inches.

2 **Oil drizzler** When pizza is served piping hot at the table, a drizzle of oil at the last minute makes it even tastier. A stainless steel oil cruet is even more attractive when it boasts a colorful handle and cap. Moreover, it's the perfect container for a spicy chili oil (made by soaking 4 to 5 dried chili peppers in olive oil).

3 **Pizza slicer** The serrated cutting edge of this implement makes for easy slicing of pizza and focaccia and also facilitates serving. Moreover, it's handy for lasagne and pies.

4 **Pizza cutting wheel** This device makes it possible to cut pizza slices without shattering the crust, even when very crispy. A hand guard makes it safe to use.

5 **Pizza plate** To bring the atmosphere of a pizzeria into your home, you may serve your pizza on large plates. This is definitely the most appropriate way of presenting pizza to your family and guests.

6 **Salt mill** An acrylic salt mill is perfect for grinding sea salt over focaccia before baking. Simply grind the salt over the surface of the dough after brushing the dough with extra-virgin olive oil.

# Glossary

### Capocollo (Calabrian coppa)
A traditional cured pork product from central-southern Italy made with the top part of the neck and part of the shoulder of the pig. Similar to coppa from Emilia, but more delicate and often more seasoned.

### Dicing
A slicing technique that requires cutting vegetables into ¼-inch cubes.

### Food processor
An invaluable appliance for mincing, mixing, pulverizing, and blending different kinds of food. A special three-blade cutting attachment, driven by a powerful electric motor, turns at thousands of revolutions per minute.

### Fior di latte mozzarella
Mozzarella cheese made from cow's milk. Low-fat versions usually have no more than 20 percent fat, while light versions have between 20–35 percent fat.

### Julienne
A slicing technique that involves cutting vegetables into very thin strips. While this technique is usually executed with a knife, a grater can also be used.

### Mandoline
A tool for cutting fruits and vegetables into a variety of different shapes (rings, julienne strips, etc.). It is called a mandoline because the hand's movements when using it are similar to those of musicians playing the musical instrument of the same name.

### Marinade
Marinades can help reduce the gamy flavor of meat and are particularly suited for many fish dishes. Red or white wine, herbs, spices, and many other seasonings can be used to prepare a marinade.

### Pasta machine
For use at home, this device, which can be electric or manual, flattens pasta dough into thin sheets and can then be used to cut the sheets into different shapes and sizes. If you don't have a pasta machine, you can roll out the dough with a rolling pin and cut with a knife.

## Pastry board

A smooth and perfectly flat marble board on which dough can be mixed, kneaded, rolled, and stretched.

## Salt flakes

Flakes of sea salt are sweeter than regular table salt, and the small crystal flakes can easily be crumbled by hand. Maldon salt is one of the most common types.

## Sprayer

This tool can be used to spray almost any liquid. Sprayers come in a range of types (gas or pump) and materials (plastic, aluminum, glass). They can be used to uniformly dampen or oil dough.

# Index

Printed in China in September 2008